First edition for the United States and Canada © copyright 1999 by Barron's Educational Series, Inc.

First edition for Great Britain published 1998 by Macdonald Young Books,
an imprint of Wayland Publishers Ltd.
Wayland is now imprint of Hodder Children's Books

Text © Pat Thomas 1998
Illustrations © Lesley Harker 1998
Volume © Hodder & Stoughton Ltd.

All inquiries should be addressed to:
Barron's Educational Series, Inc.
250 Wireless Boulevard, Hauppauge, NY 11788
http://www.barronseduc.com

Library of Congress Catalog Card No. 98-073952
ISBN-13: 978-0-7641-0995-9

Date of Manufacture : August 2011
Manufactured by : Shenzhen Wing King Tong Paper Products co.Ltd.,
Shenzhen, Guangdong, China

19 18 17 16 15 14

My Family's Changing

A FIRST LOOK AT FAMILY BREAK UP

PAT THOMAS
ILLUSTRATED BY LESLEY HARKER

BARRON'S

Something is happening in your family.
It is called divorce and you are all
going through it together.

Divorce is when
two people decide not
to be married to each
other anymore and to
live separately from
now on.

It is not your fault when your
parents get divorced, even
though it may feel like it.
It's your parent's fault, and
it's okay to feel sad and mad at
what they are doing.

When your mom and dad first met, they loved each other very much. They loved each other so much that they made a baby together.

And that baby was you.

Your parents may have hoped
that they would love each other and
live together forever. But slowly,
the way they felt about
each other changed.

The way your parents behaved towards each other changed, too. You may have noticed them doing things like disagreeing more and getting angry at each other, or not talking at all.

This is how people act when they are very unhappy with each other.

When married people are this unhappy they
often choose to divorce and not live together anymore.

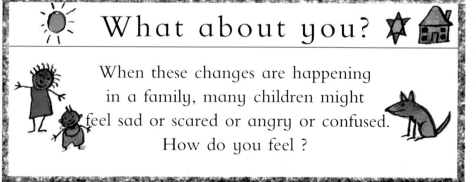

Divorce can be upsetting for the whole family, so most parents only divorce after they have tried very hard to stay together.

You may worry that when your parents stop loving each other they will stop loving you too, but this will not happen.

You may also wish that your parents would get back together again, but this does not happen often – divorce is usually forever.

Before parents get divorced, they try to decide together about things like where they will live and where you will live. You may start spending time with each of them.

When parents cannot agree about this, people called attorneys and judges decide for them. Sometimes it can take a long time to work out these decisions.

You may really miss the parent you are not living with. You may want to know what the other parent is doing and when you can get together again.

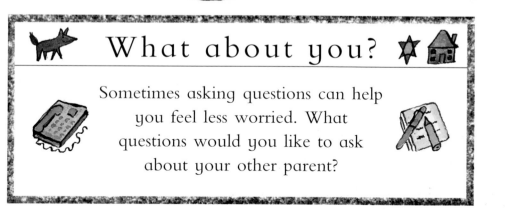

What about you?

Sometimes asking questions can help you feel less worried. What questions would you like to ask about your other parent?

Some children have overnight or weekend or vacation visits with one parent. Others might spend half their time with one and half with the other parent.

Sometimes the other parent lives far away, but you can keep in touch with them by phone or e-mail or by sending letters.

Doing things this way can feel strange at first, for all of you. It can take a while to get used to this new way of living apart.

Your parents may seem different when they are away from each other. Sometimes they are happier than before, sometimes they are sadder. They may get some new and different interests.

Often the parent you are living with seems a lot busier, because with only one grown-up in the house there is more work to do. You can help by picking up clothes and toys. You can also ask to spend more time with that parent.

Sometimes you may feel left out. Although divorce is not something that grown-ups decide to do to hurt you, you will still feel hurt. Your feelings are important, so tell your parents about them.

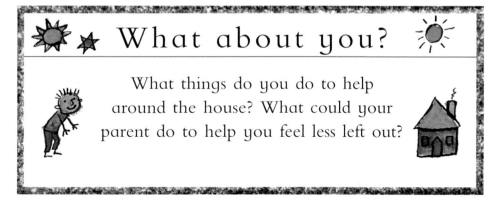

☀ ✦ What about you? ☀

What things do you do to help around the house? What could your parent do to help you feel less left out?

Spending time with other members of your family
and your friends can help you feel better.
Talking to them or to your teacher about how
you feel may be easier than talking to your parents.

Sometimes you may feel so sad
or angry that it can be
hard to talk about
it to anyone.

But it is still
important to try. Otherwise, feelings
can build up inside you, like the air inside
a balloon, until you think you are going to pop.
Or you feel very lonely because no one understands.

21

It can be upsetting to think that now your family
does not seem to be like your friends'
families or those you often see on
the television.

As you get older,
you will begin to see that there are lots of
different kinds of families. Although your parents
are divorced, they are both still a part of your family.

At first you might feel that you have to choose between your parents. But you can go on loving both of them.

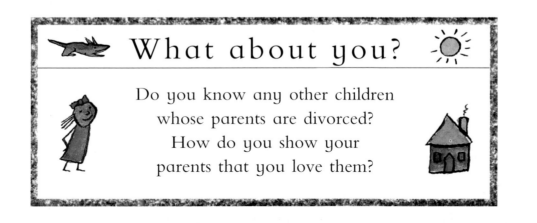

What about you?

Do you know any other children whose parents are divorced? How do you show your parents that you love them?

Sometimes parents say bad things about the other parent or buy lots of presents to make you love them more.

You may want to tell them not to do this and remind them that you enjoy being with each of them.

Sometimes you may feel upset or angry and push one of your parents away. You might do something naughty because you want to be noticed.

Your parents may tell you not to do this.

Divorce is painful for the whole family.
Each of you will have to learn
to do some things differently.

Everyone makes mistakes at first.
It is all right to make mistakes,
but we can try to learn from them.

Many things will change after your
parents' divorce, but the one thing that
will not change is their love for you.

HOW TO USE THIS BOOK

It can take a long time to talk through all there is to say about a divorce
and this book is meant to be read *with* a child, more than once.
Try reading through it first, and familiarizing yourself with its content before you begin.

Here are a few guidelines:

From time to time you will see questions within the text. These prompts are meant to give parents, teachers, and children a chance to stop and talk with each other and ask each other questions. Use the prompts when they feel right. If a child does not know how to answer, don't force the issue. You can always return to it later.

There will be plenty of time later, when the child is older, to talk about the complex whys of a divorce. Initially, the most important thing is to help the child understand what divorce is and how it will affect his or her life. A child will need lots of support in coming to terms with personal feelings about unexpected and often unwelcome changes.

Even if your divorce is for urgent reasons — such as child or spousal abuse — try not to make the mistake of assuming a child feels the same way you do. Children are very loyal and instinctively feel a need for both parents around them — even if one or both are inadequate or abusive. Go slowly and try to emphasize the benefits of getting out of such a situation.

Divorce should not be a taboo subject in school. Often this is the only place where a child may get a sense of not being alone in the experience of a family breakdown. This idea may form the basis of a useful project, such as making family trees in a collage of photographs, drawings, and words, which may also include absent or extended family members.

GLOSSARY

Divorce   the ending of a marriage by law

Feelings   We feel something through our senses, such as when we feel hot or cold. We also feel things through our emotions, such as when we feel happy or sad.

Marriage   when a man and a woman become husband and wife by law

Judge   an independent person who listens to both sides of a divorce case and decides what action should be taken

Attorney   someone who is specially trained to help parents sort out the legal details of a divorce

FURTHER READING

For Parents

Kalter, Neil. *Growing Up With Divorce*. New York: Fawcett Columbine, 1990.

Francke, Linda Bird. *Growing Up Divorced*. New York: Fawcett Crest, 1983.

Neuman, M. Gary, L.M.H.C. *Helping Your Kids Cope With Divorce*. San Francisco: Jossey-Bass Publishers,1992.

Teyber, Edward. *Helping Children Cope With Divorce*. New York: Random House, 1998.

For Parents and Children

Pickhardt, C.E. *The Case of the Scary Divorce*. Washington, DC: Magination Press, The American Psychological Association, 1997.

Thomas, Shirley, Ph.D. and Rankin, Dorthy. *Divorced But Still My Parents*. Longmont, Co: Springboard Publications,1998.

RESOURCES

Parents Without Partners
8807 Colesville Rd. Silver Springs, MD 20910
(800) 637-7974

Parents Anonymous
National Office: (909) 621-6184

The National Organization of Single Parents
P.O. Box 41522, Washington, DC 20018

Local help
Many communities offer *divorce recovery groups*. Check with your area mental health association or churches, or look in the telephone book under *Divorce*.